SP

JONES

Spooky Jokes

Illustrated by Paul Dronsfield
and Mike Phillips

p

This is a Parragon book
This edition published in 2006

Parragon
Queen Street House
4 Queen Street
Bath BA1 1HE, UK

ISBN 1-40548-096-3

Printed in China

Contents

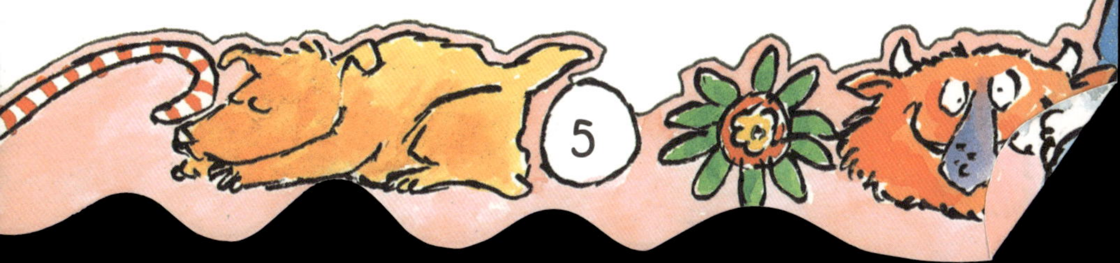

SCARY SHENANIGANS

When does a ghost
have breakfast?
In the moaning.

Why couldn't the ghost go
on the bus?
He didn't have the correct chains.

Why do ghosts shiver and moan?
**You'd do the same if you had to walk
around under a sheet all day.**

Where do spirits go for a suntan?
The Ghosta Brava.

How do you make
a milkshake?
**Sneak up behind a glass
of milk and yell, "Boo!"**

What goes, "Cackle, cackle, splat!"?
A witch flying into a lamppost.

What is a ghost's favourite bird?
A scare crow.

What does a ghost have with fish and chips?
R. I. Peas.

What's creamy and chocolaty and can read the future?
Éclair-voyant.

What does a witch's cat
say at Halloween?
"Trick or trout?"

Where do baby ghosts go
during the day?
Dayscare centres.

What's the most important
programme on a witch's computer?
The spell checker.

What do you call an owl with a toupee?
Hedwig.

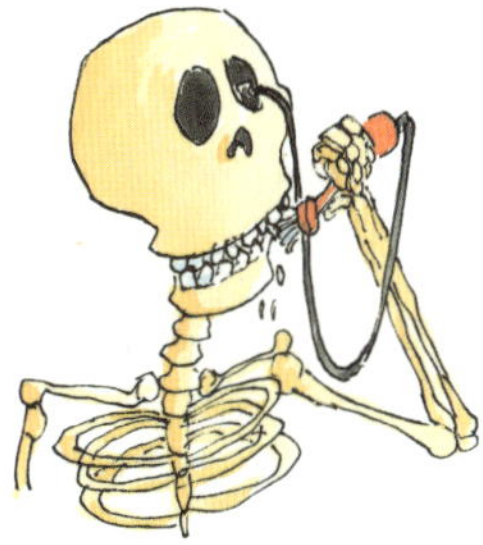

What do you get when you cross Bambi with a ghost?
Bamboo.

What trees do witches plant in their gardens?
Brooms.

What should you say when you meet a ghost?
"How do you boo, sir, how do you boo?"

What goes, "Cackle, cackle, crackle."?
A witch spontaneously combusting.

Where do witches have
their temples?
Either side of their head.

What did the mother ghost
say to the baby ghost?
"Put your boos and shocks on."

What story do little ghosts like
to hear at bedtime?
Ghouldilocks and the three scares.

Who's in charge of the ghost detectives?
The chief inspectre.

Why couldn't the witch fly for long distances?
She got broomsick.

How do ghosts keep fit?
By regular exorcise.

What do ghosts drink at breakfast?
Coffee with scream and sugar.

What's the difference between a witch and the letters m, a, k, e and s?
One makes spells and the other spells makes.

Why did the wizard get into the fridge?
He was in for a cold spell.

Who do witches share
flats with?
Their broommates.

What vehicle does a kid ghost like
to ride?
A boocycle.

When do ghosts go to work?
Moandays to Frightdays.

Did you hear about the
Daffy Duck witch?
She kept having Disney spells.

What are a ghouls
best friend?
Demons.

What do ghosts eat for dinner?
Spook-ghetti.

What's the best way to imagine you're
flying on a broomstick?
Witchful thinking.

Where do phantoms mail
their letters?
At the ghost office.

Where does a ghost go on
Saturday night?
Anywhere where he can boo-gie.

What time is it when a ghost haunts your
house?
Time to move to a new house.

How many witches does it take to change
a light bulb?
**It depends what you want them
to change it into.**

Which wizard never goes to the barber?
Hairy Potter.

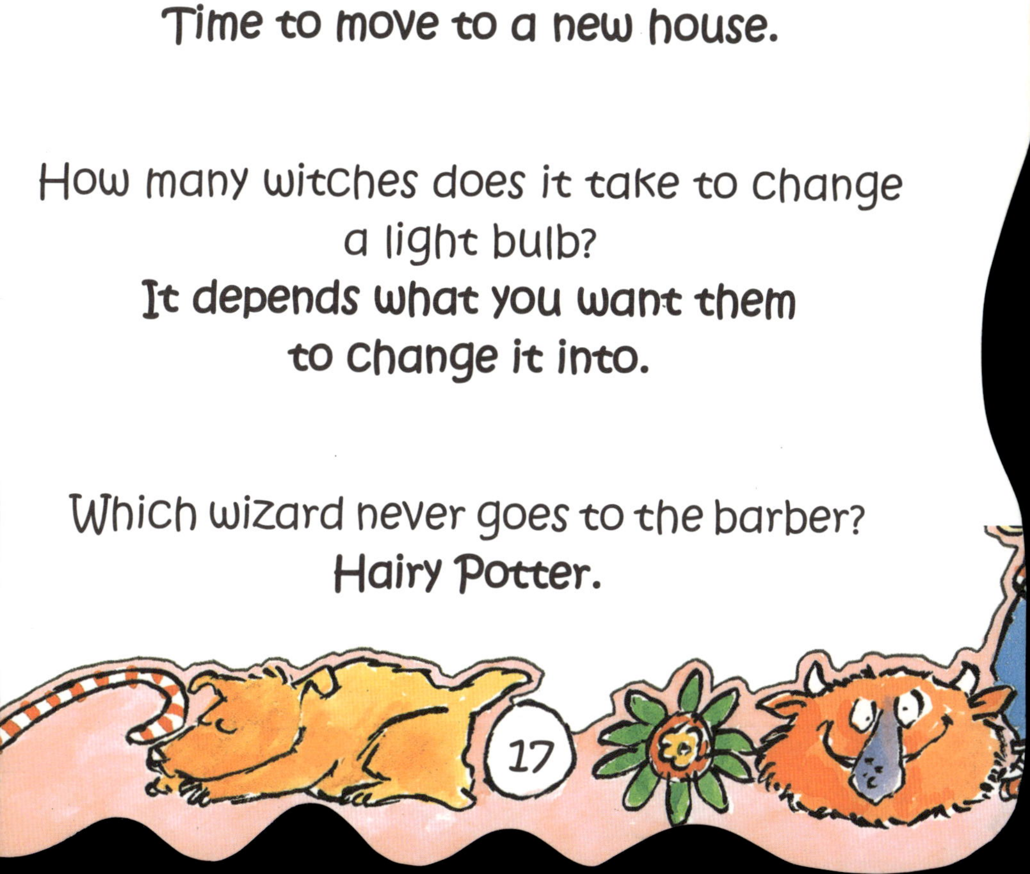

What do you get if you
cross a cocker spaniel,
a poodle and a ghost?
A cocker-poodle-boo.

Why did the witch take a week to
make a spell?
It was a slow-motion-potion.

How do ghosts start their cars?
With spook plugs.

What do you call a wizard with
dandruff?
A blizzard.

What happens when a ghost gets lost in the fog?
He is mist.

What do ghosts use to wash their hair?
Sham-boo.

What do ghosts drink with their meals?
Whine.

Why couldn't the ghost get a whisky in the pub?
They didn't serve spirits.

How can you tell when
a window is scared?
It gets shudders.

What do phantoms do when they need
more coffee on a plane?
**Call the air ghostess or the
fright attendant.**

Why did the wizard wear a pointed hat?
Because he had a pointed head.

What kind of sorceress lives by
the sea?
A sandwitch.

What did the witch say
to her cat?
"You're familiar."

What happens when ghosts
haunt a theatre?
The actors get stage fright.

What is Beethoven doing in his
coffin right now?
Decomposing.

What kind of sorceress lives by the
sea but is afraid to go swimming?
A chicken sandwitch.

Who is the most famous
ghost detective?
Sherlock Moans.

Who is the most famous skeleton
detective?
Sherlock Bones.

Who is the most famous wizard
detective?
Warlock Holmes.

What do witches take to the beach?
Suntan potion.

Why do ghosts love pubs?

Because of all the boos.

Why was the weather witch
so popular?
**She was always forecasting
sunny spells.**

What do you call a haunted chicken?
A poultry-geist.

What do Hawaiian ghosts play?
The spookulele.

Where do ghosts do their homework?
Exorcise books.

How does a wizard's cooking pot introduce itself?
"Hello, I'm called Ron."

What do you call a spirit novelist?
A ghost writer.

What do you call a spirit playwright?
A crypt writer.

What kind of witch speeds down the motorway at 100mph?
A road hag.

Why did the wizard make his potions in a cauldron?
His microwave was on the blink.

What does a formula-one witch ride?
A vrooomstick.

What does a witch do when she goes on a diet?
She joins weight witches.

What are baby witches called?
Halloweenies.

Why do little witches come top of the class?
Because they're so good at spelling.

How should you talk to an evil, ugly witch?
By long-distance phone call.

What two items do witches need for the perfect meal?
Hansel and griddle.

Why is the air so fresh and clean at Halloween?
Because of the witches sweeping the sky.

What do spooks chant at football matches?

"Here we ghost, here we ghost, here we ghost..."

Why did the witch
poison the boy's cornflakes?
She was a cereal killer

What did the teacher witch do to
her terrible pupil?
Ex-spelled her.

What's the difference between a deer
on the run and a miniature witch?
**One's a hunted stag and the
other's a stunted hag.**

What do witches sell in art shops?
Witch craft.

For what crime are ghosts
most often sent to prison?
Booglary.

Why did the witch's cat always go
to the wizard?
Because sorcerers are often filled with milk.

What kind of make-up do ghosts wear?
Mas-scare-a.

Why don't witches get angry when
they're on a broomstick?
They don't want to fly off the handle.

Why did the wizard jump
off Nelson's Column?
**He wanted to be a big hit in
the West End.**

What do ghosts play when they're bored?
Moanopoly.

How can you make a tall witch short?
Borrow all her money.

Who protects the shores
where spirits live?
The ghostguard.

Why is a witch like a candle?
They are both wicked.

What do baby ghosts wear?
Pillowcases.

Why did the gravedigger steal knickers?
Because he wanted to be an undie-taker.

Why was the woman in love with the ghost?
She was possessed.

What does a ghost have on
top of his apple pie?
Whipped scream.

What kind of music do ghosts like?
Rhythm and boos.

How do you make a witch float?
**Get a couple of scoops of ice cream,
some lemonade and a witch.**

What kind of play do ghosts like
to see at Christmas time?
A phantomime.

TROUBLESOME TIKES

What does a cannibal get
when he comes home late
for dinner?
The cold shoulder.

Did you hear about the cannibal boy
who was 8 before he was 7?
It's very sad he went so young.

What instrument do skeletons play?
The trombone.

Why do witches have stiff joints?
They get broomatism!

What did the cannibal do
on the cruise boat?
Told the captain to take the menu away and bring the passenger list.

Did you hear about the cannibal that
passed his friend on the high street?
He was fined £100 for fouling the pavement.

Why don't skeletons play music in church?
They don't have any organs.

What do you call an adolescent skeleton?
A skeleteen.

What did the skeleton say
to the barman?
"A pint of beer and a mop, please."

Why shouldn't a cannibal eat
eyeballs and brain on an empty stomach?
It's more polite to use a plate.

Why was the skeleton so thirsty?
He was bone dry.

Did you hear about the cannibal who
loved Italian food?
He ordered a pizza with everybody on it.

Why did the sorceress buy a huge mansion?
Because she was so witch.

Why wouldn't the skeleton get a job?
He was bone idle.

What do cannibals eat for pudding?
Chocolate-covered aunts.

What kind of wine does a skeleton like?
One with plenty of body.

Why do skeletons wear
thick coats?
**If they don't, the wind goes
straight through them.**

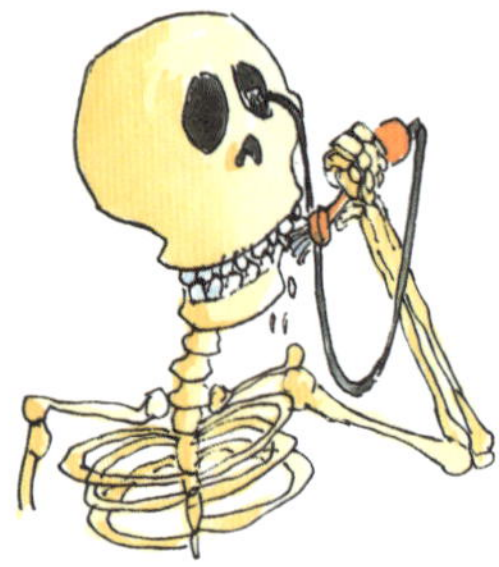

What's a cannibal's
favourite game?
Swallow the leader.

Why did the skeleton call off
the wedding?
His heart wasn't in it.

What do you call a stupid skeleton?
Bonehead.

How did the sick witch
get to hospital?
She flu.

Have you ever been to a cannibal department store?
No, everything costs an arm and a leg.

Why do skeletons hate parties?
They get used as coat hangers.

What did the cannibal say to the famous explorer?
"Dr Livingstone, I consume?"

What do skeletons use for crockery?
Bone china.

Why did the skeleton go to jail?
He was bad to the bone.

Why didn't the cannibal like eating the clown?
He thought it tasted funny.

What do you say to terrify a skeleton?
"Here, Fido, din-dins!"

What does a cannibal eat with cheese?
Pickled organs.

Why was the cannibal
expelled from school?
He kept buttering up the teacher.

Which skeleton was defeated at
the Battle of Waterloo?
Napoleon Bonyparts.

What did the cannibal say after his wife
made a good meal?
"I'm really going to miss her."

Why are skeletons so calm?
Because nothing gets under their skin.

What do skeletons say
before the start of a meal?
"Bone appétit."

What happened to the commander who was put in the chief cannibal's cooking pot?
He became commander-in-chief.

What do cannibals do to their toughest foes?
Stick them in the microwave until they're tender.

What kind of art do skeletons like?
Skullture.

How does a skeleton stop?
Vertebrakes.

How did the skeleton know
the cannibal was up to no good?
He could feel it in his bones.

What did the cannibal do in an
"all you can eat" restaurant?
He ate two waiters and the chef.

What do you get if you cross a skeleton
with a jar of peanut butter?
Extra-crunchy peanut butter.

What's the definition of a cannibal?
**Someone who loves his fellow
man – with gravy.**

Why do you have to wait so long for a ghost train?

They only operate a skeleton service.

Why couldn't the cannibal boil the missionary in his pot?

Because he was a friar.

Why aren't there any famous skeletons?

Because they're such a bunch of nobodies.

How did skeletons in the Wild West get their mail?

The bony express.

How can you help a
hungry cannibal?
Give him a hand.

Why are cemeteries always such noisy places?
All the coffin.

What do cannibals call a line
of people waiting at a bus stop?
A barbequeue.

How do you reach a skeleton
when he's not at home?
Call his mobile bone.

What's a skeleton's favourite
kind of apple?
Coccyx.

What's a skeleton's favourite fruit?
Bone-anas.

What vegetable do skeletons
like more than any other?
Marrow.

Why did the cannibal's daughter
go to so many parties?
She was looking for an edible bachelor.

Why was the Scandinavian cannibal vegetarian?
He would only eat swedes.

How can you tell the difference between a male and a female skeleton?
She's the one with the diamond ring.

Who is a skeleton's favourite pop star?
Bone-o.

What's the definition of a shocking noise?
A skeleton dancing on a tin roof.

What did the cannibal say
when he was full?
"I couldn't eat another mortal!"

How do you spot a polite ghost?
It only spooks when spoken to.

Why didn't the scarecrow
ever have any fun?
He was a stuffed shirt.

How do undertakers speak?
Gravely.

Why did the skeleton go
to the disco?
He heard it was a hip joint.

What do cannibals do
if their slaves are revolting?
Skip that course and have pudding.

Did you hear about the skeleton postman?
A dog ran off with some bones and he didn't have a leg to stand on.

What did the skeleton say when
he won the competition?
Hip, hip, hooray.

Why did the cannibal feel sick?
He ate someone who disagreed with him.

What sort of books do skeletons like?
Spine chillers.

Why did the cannibal come back from holiday with no arms or legs?
It was self-catering.

What made the moon pale?
The atmos-fear.

Why don't skeletons get along?
They've always got bones to pick with each other.

What happens if you upset a cannibal?
You get into hot water.

Who was the skeleton in the cupboard?
The winner of the great hide-and-seek competition of 1906.

What's huge, red and swims in the ocean?
Moby Bus.

Why did the cannibal get told off by his mother after he joked with a friend?
Because he was playing with his food.

What's a skeleton's favourite quotation?
"Tibia or not tibia, that is the question."

Who is the skeleton king of rock and roll?
Pelvis.

How do ghosts get out of the cemetery when it's locked?
They use a skeleton key.

What did the cannibal make of his new boss?
A casserole.

Why should you never
believe a skeleton?
**They're always telling fibulas,
and you can see right through them.**

What happened to the cannibal lion?
He swallowed his pride.

Why should you never fight a skeleton?
He'll stab you with his shoulder blades.

What happened to the boat that sank
in the shark-infested sea?
It came back with a skeleton crew.

What's a cannibal's
favourite fast food snack?
A handburger.

Why do skeletons get away with murder?
The police can't pin anything on them.

Why did the cannibal catch a viper
and dwarf?
He fancied a snake and pygmy pie.

What happened to the man who
didn't pay the exorcist's bill?
He was repossessed.

What sort of jokes do
skeletons like?
Rib ticklers.

What did the cannibal say at
his sugar plantation?
"I'll feed my lads with m'lasses!"

What do skeletons give their
girlfriends on Valentine's Day?
Bone-bones in a heart-shaped box.

Why were the skeletons so happy
after the party?
They had a rattling good time.

IMPISH INCIDENTS

Do zombies eat popcorn
with their fingers?
No, they eat the fingers separately.

What is a vampire's favourite sport?
Casketball.

Why does an imp get indigestion?
Goblin his food.

Why doesn't Dracula have
any friends?
He's a pain in the neck.

What's a vampire's
favourite fast food?
**Someone with very high
blood pressure.**

Why did the witch feed her cat pennies?
**She wanted to put some
money in the kitty.**

What does a ghoul eat for breakfast?
Rice Creepies.

What do you get if you cross
a vampire and a pygmy?
A pain in the knee.

What should you do
if you like Dracula?
Join his fang club.

How do you join
Dracula's fang club?
**Send your name,
address and blood group.**

What did the vampire say to his victim?
"Your neck's on my list!"

Why was the vampire heartbroken?
His love was in vein.

What did the vampire say when
he saw a victim sleeping peacefully?
"Ahh! Breakfast in bed!"

What do young zombies
call their parents?
Mummy and Deady.

How did the vampire slayer make holy water?
**She took some tap water and boiled
the hell out of it.**

What did Grandpa Ghoul say to his grandson
when he hadn't seen him for ages?
"You gruesome!"

Why do vampires drink blood?
Fizzy drinks are bad for their fangs.

What on earth is as sharp as a vampire's fang?
His other fang.

Why do vampires love school dinners?
They know they won't get steak.

What does a vampire fear most?
Tooth decay.

Why did Dracula take up acting?
It was in his blood.

Where did they put Dracula
when he was arrested?
In a blood cell.

What do you give vampires with sore throats?
Coffin medicine.

What should you do if a zombie
rolls his eyes at you?
Pick them up and roll them back.

What groups do vampires join?
Blood groups.

What are Dracula's
favourite fruits?
Neck-tarines.

What's the difference between a lunatic
shouting fish names and vampires?
**One states, "Hake!" and the others
hate stakes.**

Why is it so hard to ask Dracula
for a dance?
**As soon as he's finished the
fangdango, he goes into the vaults.**

How do devils protest?
In demon-strations.

What did the mummy vampire say to her screaming baby?
"Stop crying, you're driving me batty."

What happened when two rival vampire sects started fighting?
Fang warfare.

What is Dracula's favourite cocktail?
A Bloody Mary.

What's Dracula's favourite soup?
Scream of tomato.

When do vampires bite you?
On wincedays.

What do you get if you cross
a werewolf and a vampire?
A fur coat that fangs around your neck.

What do vampires love to have
for pudding?
Knickerbocker ghouly.

What do elves learn at school?
The elfabet.

What do you get if you cross
a vampire and a mummy?
A gift-wrapped bat.

What's the best way to get rid of demons?
Plenty of exorcise.

Where do zombies stay on holiday?
**Anywhere that there's running rot
and mould in every room.**

What does the baby vampire say before going to bed?
"Turn on the dark. I'm afraid of the light."

What TV sitcom do demons never miss?
Fiends.

What does Dracula sing in the shower?
Fang you for the music.

Why do vampires take up skateboarding?
They think it's really ghoul, man.

What do you call
a bloodsucker who enjoys
sleeping in the great
outdoors?
A campfire vampire.

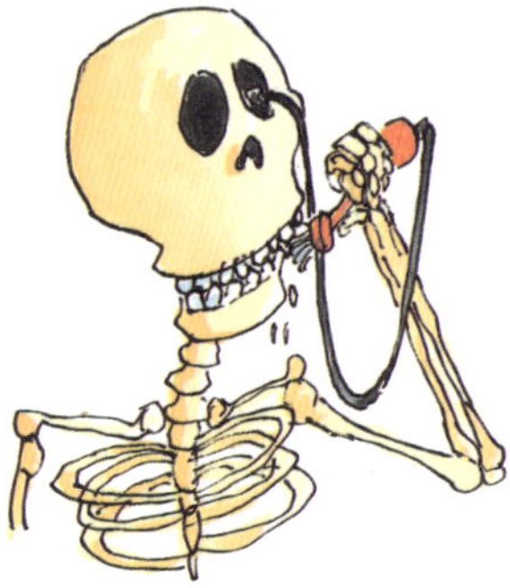

Why do vampires have such good marriages?
They're batty about each other.

What do demons say when they meet in the morning?
"How the devil are you?"

Where do vampires keep their savings?
In blood banks.

What do zombies wear in the rain?
Ca-ghouls.

Why is everybody bored of Dracula's artwork?

Because he always draws blood.

How do you know if a vampiress likes you?

She bats her eyes.

How do vampires cross the English Channel?

Blood vessels.

Did you hear about the boxer who went looking for Dracula?

He was out for the count.

Who's the captain of the graveyard football team?
The ghoulie.

What position do zombies play at netball?
Ghoul shooter.

Why do demons and ghouls get on so well?
Because demons are a ghoul's best friend.

What kind of coffee do vampires order?
Decoffinated.

What do vampire footballers have at half-time?
Blood oranges.

What happened when the vampire bit a goose?
He felt down in the mouth.

Why can't vampires gamble?
They run away when anyone puts forward a stake.

Why did the football manager sign a horrible, blood-sucking beast?
Because his team needed a ghoul to win.

Why did the vampire come top of the class?
Because he passed his blood test.

Who has the most dangerous job in Transylvania?
Dracula's dentist.

Why are monsters
covered in wrinkles?
Have you ever tried to iron a monster?

What type of imp is an excellent cook?
A hobgoblin.

What did the teacher say
to Dracula after he failed his
maths exam?
"Can't you Count Dracula?"

Why don't vampires argue?
Because they'd make themselves cross.

What do ghouls play during break time?
Corpse and robbers.

What's the first thing a vampire bites after he gets his teeth checked?
The dentist.

What kind of vampire only bites people when they aren't looking.
A shy one.

Why do vampires have lentils, chickpeas and beans with their meals?
Because they'll eat anything with pulses.

Why do zombies love mazes?
All the dead ends.

Why are zombies so tired all the time?
They're dead on their feet.

What do you get if you cross a vampire with a 24-hour clock?
An all-day sucker.

Why is Dracula such
a successful gymnast?
He loves the vault.

How did the vampire cure his sore throat?
By gargoyling.

What comes out after dark and goes,
"Chomp, suck, ouch!"?
A vampire with a rotten tooth.

What did Godzilla say after he had
eaten London?
"What's for dinner?"

How can you tell if you've been bitten by a vampire?
Every time you have a drink, your neck leaks.

Why did Dracula recruit
an apprentice?
**He thought he could do with
some new blood.**

Why do vampires make
blood-curdling screams?
**They're too runny to spread on their
toast otherwise.**

What would happen to a mummy if it
fell in the River Nile?
It would get wet.

Why is Cinderella so
bad at sport?
Because her coach was a pumpkin.

How many zombies can you get into
an empty grave?
Only one – then it's not empty any more.

What's woolly, has four legs, goes
baaa and sucks blood?
A lambpire.

MONSTER MUNCH

Why did the monster eat
a light bulb?
He fancied a light snack.

Why do dragons sleep during the day?
So they can fight knights.

How do you stop a monster biting his nails?
Give him a bag of screws to chew on.

Why was the monster with sixteen
hands but no feet so clumsy?
He was all fingers and thumbs.

What's a monster's
favourite play?
Romeo and Ghouliet.

What does Quasimodo use
to iron his clothes?
A wok.

What does a slavering twenty-storey
monster eat?
Anything it likes.

How can you tell that a monster's
been in your bathroom?
The top's been left off the toothpaste.

Did you hear about the werewolf that went bald in the war?

It happened in a hair raid.

Why was the little Egyptian boy so upset?

His daddy was a mummy.

What's the difference between a smelly, slimy monster and strawberries?

Everyone likes strawberries.

What monster has never won the lottery?

The Luck Less Monster.

Why did the Cyclops have
to close his school?
He only had one pupil.

What kind of monster has
the most ears?
The eeriest.

What do you call a monster with no neck?
The Lost Neck Monster.

What time is it if a monster steps
on your car?
Time to buy a new one.

How do you get a dozen monsters
in a chocolate box?
Take the chocolates out first.

What monster goes around ruffling people's hair?
The Locks Mess Monster.

Where do mummies go swimming?
The Dead Sea.

Why did the headless horseman go into business?
He wanted to get ahead in life.

What did Quasimodo shout to the kids chasing him down the road?
"I tell you, I don't have your football!"

Did you hear about the man
who used to be a werewolf?
He's much better nooooooooow!

How do we know that Dr Frankenstein
was a very funny man?
He had his monster in stitches.

Why did Frankenstein stick his
finger in the plug socket?
He was interested in current events.

Where do you find monster snails?
On the end of monsters' fingers.

What kind of monster has one eye and rides a bike?
Cycle-ops.

How do you raise a baby monster that's been abandoned by its parents?
With a crane.

What did the monster say when he came home with a sack full of gnus?
"Have I got gnus for you!"

Why was Dr Frankenstein so popular?
He was an expert at making new friends.

Why is Frankenstein's
monster so easily agitated?

**Because he has
amps in his pants.**

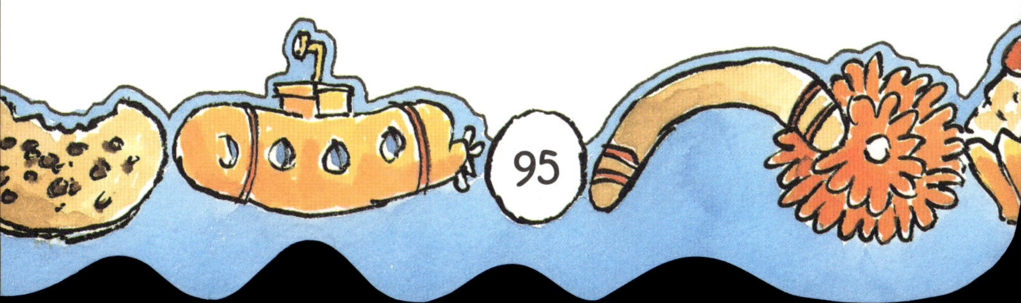

Why couldn't Swamp Thing go to the party?
Because he was bogged down at work.

What do you call a yeti that does a hundred sit-ups a day?
The abdominal snowman.

What do you call a yeti that's always late?
The abominable slowman.

What do mummies use for make up?
Nile varnish.

What do sea monsters eat?
Fish and ships.

Why did the vicar call the werewolf "Fixit"?
He kept doing little jobs around the churchyard.

Where does King Kong sit in the cinema?
Anywhere he likes.

What's hairy and hangs off the Empire State Building stinking of rotten eggs?
King Pong.

What's the best way to get in touch with a sea monster?
Drop it a line.

Did you hear about the monster with five legs?
His trousers fit him like a glove.

How do you make a werewolf stew?
Keep it waiting for a few hours.

What is terrifying, hairy and drinks from the wrong side of the glass?
A werewolf with hiccups.

Why does Frankenstein's
monster get indigestion?
He bolts down his food.

Why was the sea monster so upset?
The sea weed.

Why did the monster leave the table?
**He'd already eaten the fridge,
the cooker and the kitchen cabinets.**

What invention enabled
Dr Frankenstein to walk through walls?
The door.

What do monsters call
children on roller blades?
Meals on wheels.

What should you do if a werewolf bites
your foot off?
**Keep out of the kitchen – you'll make
a terrible mess on that clean floor.**

What sort of music do mummies like best?
Wrap.

Where do werewolves live?
Werehouses.

What's wrapped in cling
film and terrorizes Paris?
The lunch-pack of Notre Dame.

How does a werewolf sign off his letters?
Best vicious.

What giant monster goose terrorizes China?
Honk Kong.

What's green, very tall and mopes
in the corner?
The Incredible Sulk.

What happened when the
werewolf swallowed a clock?
He got ticks.

Why can't mummies make friends?
They're too wrapped up in themselves.

How do you know if the bogeyman
is in your house?
All the tissues are missing.

How do you stop a monster digging up
your garden?
Take his spade away.

Why was the boy so upset to
find a monster in his bath?
It had used all the hot water.

Why did the mummy leave his tomb after
five thousand years?
He was old enough to leave home.

Why is a dirty werewolf like a camera?
It snaps and makes prints.

Why did the vampire cross the road?
To bite someone on the other side.

What's the difference between a werewolf and a cucumber?

I won't be asking you to do my shopping, if you don't know.

How does a werewolf move?
In vicious circles.

Why did the invisible man look in the mirror?
He wanted to make sure he wasn't there.

Did you hear about the
monster that had an eye for the ladies?
He kept it in his back pocket.

What happened to the monster that
took the five o'clock train home?
He had to give it back.

Why shouldn't you let a werewolf into your house?
They leave hairs all over the sofa.

Why do monsters hunt in sewers?
They love convenience food.

What do you get if King Kong steps on Batman and Robin?
Flatman and Ribbon.

What should you do if a monster borrows your bicycle?
Let him take it for as long as he wants.

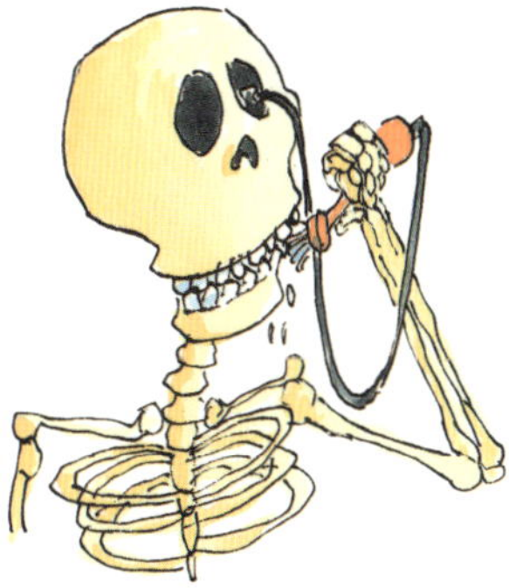

What happens if you cross
a werewolf and a sheep?
You have to get a new sheep.

What do you get when King Kong
walks through your vegetable patch?
Squash

Why did the monster relish Chinese boats?
He loved eating junk food.

What do monsters eat for breakfast?
Ham and legs.

What business is King Kong in?
Monkey business.

What sort of fur do you get
from a werewolf?
As fur away as possible.

Why shouldn't you yank a werewolf's tail?
**It might be a werewolf's tail,
but it's surely the end of you.**

What is even more invisible than
the invisible man?
The invisible man's shadow.

What has two wheels, ten
arms, five heads and a bell?
A monster on a bicycle.

How scared was the little dog
when it saw a monster?
Terrierfied.

How did the hideous mutant monster
count to 112?
On his fingers.

What do monsters call busy swimming pools?
Soup.

What do you get if King Kong
falls down a mine shaft?
A flat miner.

What do you call a ten-foot monster
with tentacles and razor-sharp teeth?
"Your most wondrous majesty!"

What do monsters use when they shop?
Body bags.

What do you get if you cross
a werewolf with a hyena?
**I don't know but if it laughs
you'd better join in.**

What do you get if you cross King Kong with a snowman?

Frostbite.

What's huge, grey and puffy, hovers over London and eats people?

A cloud. I was lying about the eating people part.

What game do monsters like to play at parties?

Hide and shriek.